PROPERTY OF
BOGOTA PUBLIC LIBRARY
BOGOTA, N.J. 07603

compiled by
Penrose Colyer

Italian by
Adriana Giussani

illustrated by
Colin Mier
and Wendy Lewis

Franklin Watts
NEW YORK · TORONTO 1983

I Can Read
ITALIAN
My First English~Italian Word Book

Contents

9	Reading and talking Italian
10	How many? *Quanti?*
12	Timothy's friends *Gli amici di Timoteo*
16	Timothy has a bath *Timoteo fa il bagno*
18	They want to be... *Vorrebbero essere...*
20	At the zoo *Allo zoo*
22	George and Genevieve *Giorgio e Genoveffa*
24	At the cinema *Al cinema*
26	Where do they live? *Dove abitano?*
28	Mr. Smith in the kitchen *Il signor Smith in cucina*
30	Timothy in hospital *Timoteo all'ospedale*
32	From the helicopter *Dall'elicottero*
34	If I were a millionaire... *Se fossi un miliardario...*
36	Swimming *Il nuoto*
38	Timothy looks at television *Timoteo guarda la televisione*
40	Marion Scott at school *Marianna Scott a scuola*
42	Who has walked this way? *Chi è passato di qui?*
44	Jeremy the gipsy goes to bed *Geremia, lo zingaro, va a letto*
46	Mrs. Brown's cake *La torta della signora Brown*

First published in the UK by Eurobook Limited
First published in the USA in 1983 by Franklin Watts
387 Park Avenue South New York New York 10016

Copyright © 1972 by Eurobook Limited
Italian text © 1973 by Vallecchi Editore, Firenze
All rights reserved throughout the world.
No part of this publication may be reproduced,
stored in a retrieval system or transmitted,
in any form or by any means, electronic, mechanical,
photocopying, recording or otherwise, without the
prior written permission of Eurobook Limited.

ISBN 0-531-04601-X
Printed in Spain by Graficas Reunidas SA

48	**In the garden early in the morning** *In giardino al mattino presto*	82	**Skeletons** *Scheletri*
50	**Presents** *Regali*	84	**On the escalator** *Sulla scala mobile*
52	**In the chocolate factory** *Nella fabbrica di cioccolatini*	86	**Mrs. Brown and Timothy make bread** *La signora Brown e Timoteo fanno il pane*
54	**Timothy and John go to a football match** *Timoteo e Gianni vanno alla partita*	88	**My family** *La mia famiglia*
56	**Timothy at the seaside** *Timoteo al mare*	90	**I like eating ...** *Mi piace mangiare ...*
58	**On holiday** *In vacanza*	92	**Peter the astronaut's birthday** *Il compleanno di Piero l'astronauta*
60	**At the hairdresser's** *Dal parrucchiere*	94	**Jeremy goes to the races** *Geremia va alle corse*
62	**Miss Miller buys a dog** *La signorina Miller compra un cane*	96	**Timothy in a hovercraft** *Timoteo in aliscafo*
64	**The hockey match** *La partita di hockey*	98	**House for sale** *Casa in vendita*
66	**I'm going to be ...** *Diventerò ...*	100	**In an office** *In un ufficio*
68	**A concert** *Un concerto*	102	**Big buildings** *Grandi edifici*
70	**Timothy goes to the Motor Show** *Timoteo va al Salone dell'Automobile*	104	**At the airport** *All'aeroporto*
72	**In the playground** *Al parco giochi*	106	**The burglars** *I ladri*
74	**Parents and children** *Genitori e bambini*	108	**At the wax museum** *Al museo delle cere*
76	**Peter goes to the moon** *Piero va sulla luna*	110	**How do they get around?** *Come viaggiano?*
78	**Mrs. Brown chooses a hat** *La signora Brown sceglie un cappello*	112	**At the Scotts' house in the evening** *La sera in casa Scott*
80	**At the ice-rink** *Sulla pista di pattinaggio*	114	**Do you know?** *Lo sai?*
		116	**A page for parents**

Reading Italian

In Italy you read Italian wherever you go—and without looking at a single book. There are names of Italian shops, such as **macelleria** (butcher's), **farmacia** (chemist's), and **profumeria** (shop that sells perfume and toiletries); signposts such as **Roma 100** (Rome 100 kilometres), and advertisements for Italian things. In order to get around and know what to do you have to be able to read signs such as **entrata** (entrance) and **uscita** (exit), **vietato fumare** (no smoking), è **pericoloso sporgersi dal finestrino** (it is dangerous to lean out of the window), **gabinetti** (toilets) and many others.

So when you go to Italy, as you probably will one day, it is important that you should be able to read Italian. And even if you never go to Italy you can read Italian books and magazines which can be bought in your own country.

With this book you can practise reading Italian. If you are learning it at school, you will probably know some of the words already; and you will learn some new ones too. Some Italian words are very similar to English ones, either in the way they are spelt or in the way they are spoken; you will have fun when you find that **famiglia** (pronounced fameelya) means family; **animali** (pronounced animahlee) animals, **lezione** (pronounced letsiohnay) lesson and **cioccolato** (pronounced chokkolahtoh) chocolate. Many words appear again and again, so that by the time you get to the end of the book you will know them well.

Talking Italian

Talking Italian means not only saying Italian words but also making Italian sounds. Some of the sounds of Italian are the same as English ones, but many are rather different; the only way to be able to say them correctly is by listening hard to Italian people talking and trying to imitate the sounds they make.

The main difference is that Italian vowel sounds are very pure. Each vowel is pronounced very clearly and distinctly wherever it occurs in the word.

The other important thing to know is that all Italian words of two or more syllables are stressed somewhere. The stress usually comes on the second-to-last syllable as in the words **amici** (friends), pronounced ameèchee and **professore** (professor), pronounced professòray. But sometimes it comes in other places such as the beginning of the word, as in **zingaro** (gypsy), pronounced zìngahroh.

The following words, which all appear in the book, contain many of the Italian sounds and combinations of letters that are different from those you use in English. Under each word there is a guide to how to say it. We have also marked each word with a stress mark (`) above the syllable or part of the word that you must stress as you say it to yourself.

quanti: how many
kwàntee: kwant to rhyme with "ant".

bottiglie: bottles
bottèeleeay

draghi: dragons
dràghee

lezioni: lessons
letsiòhnee

lettura: reading
lettòorah

amici: friends
amèechee

ti piace?: do you like?
tee peeahchay?

Giorgio: George
Jòrjoh

gelato: ice-cream
jellàhtoh

leggere: to read
lèjjeray

occhi: eyes
òkkee

anche: also
ànkay

righello: ruler
reegèlloh: hard g as in "get".

dimagrisce: she is getting thin
deemahgrèeshay

pesci: fish
pàyshee

maschera: usherette
màskairah

signora: Mrs
seenyòrah

Piero: Peter
Peeàiroh

paesi: countries
pahyàyzee

ciao: hello
chow: to rhyme with "now".

suoi: his, her
swòyee

isola: island
eèzohlah

hanno: they have
ànnoh

cioccolato: chocolate
chokkohlàhtoh

Three final things to remember are that the letter h is never pronounced; that you can make yourself sound more Italian if you trill your r's; that the combination of letters *gl* followed by *i* is pronounced rather like the double *ll* in "million".

Perhaps all this sounds rather complicated, but understanding what people mean is not always as difficult as you might expect. An Italian shows what he means not only by the words he says, but by his whole face, his hands and sometimes his whole body too. His eyebrows shoot up when he asks a question and his mouth stretches wide open; his hands point to himself or to someone else as he talks about them. Without understanding the words, it is often quite easy to understand what an Italian is saying, just by looking at him.

When you listen, do not try to pick out each single word that is said. You would find that difficult to do anyway because Italian people tend to talk very fast and run words into one another. Try instead to get an idea of the sort of sounds which are made. Try also to tell what a whole sentence sounds like and get a general idea of what is being said.

If you cannot listen to or watch an Italian person (a real one, or one on television or in a film), listen to a record of Italian being spoken or sung.

How many?
Quanti?

Four bottles of Coca-Cola
Quattro bottiglie di Coca-Cola

Do you like Coca-Cola?
Ti piace la Coca-Cola?

Six umbrellas
Sei ombrelli

How many raindrops are there?
Quante gocce di pioggia ci sono?

Three giraffes
Tre giraffe

How many eyes have they?
Quanti occhi hanno?

And how many spots?
E quante chiazze?

A hundred?
Cento?

Two large dragons
Due grossi draghi

One island
Un'isola

How many people are there on the island?
Quante persone ci sono sull'isola?

Candles
Candeline

It's somebody's birthday.
È il compleanno di qualcuno.

He is nine.
Ha nove anni.

Ten goldfish
Dieci pesci rossi

Five lucky horseshoes
Cinque ferri di cavallo porta-fortuna

Is this man lucky?
Quest'uomo è fortunato?

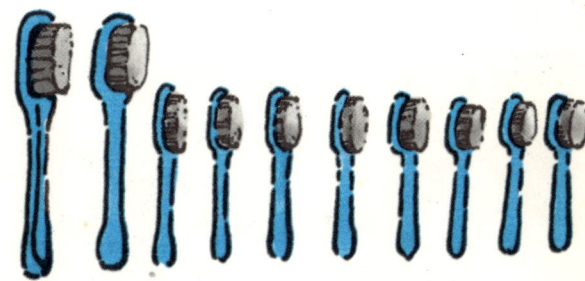

The toothbrushes of a large family
Gli spazzolini da denti di una famiglia numerosa

There are eight children in the family.
In famiglia ci sono otto bambini.

Here are seven men.
Ecco sette uomini.

There are three cowboys and four gangsters.
Ci sono tre cowboy e quattro fuorilegge.

Who is winning?
Chi vince?

Henry Smith
Enrico Smith

Maurice, Timothy's parrot
Maurizio, il pappagallo di Timoteo

George, the keeper at the zoo
Giorgio, il guardiano dello zoo

Timothy's

Mr. Smith
Il signor Smith

Mrs. Brown
La signora Brown

Bob, the dog
Bob, il cane

Miss Miller
La signorina Miller

John
Gianni

Timothy's friends
Gli amici di Timoteo

Timothy is a tramp.
Timoteo è un vagabondo.
He is also the hero of this book.
È anche il protagonista di questo libro.
Here are some of his friends.
Ecco qui alcuni suoi amici.

Maurice is Timothy's parrot.
Maurizio è il pappagallo di Timoteo.
He has green feathers.
Ha le piume verdi.
He is very proud of his feathers.
È molto orgoglioso delle sue piume.

Albert is Timothy's cat.
Alberto è il gatto di Timoteo.
In summer, Albert stays with Timothy.
D'estate Alberto sta con Timoteo.
But in winter it's cold.
Ma d'inverno fa freddo.
Albert doesn't like the cold.
Ad Alberto non piace il freddo.
In winter, Albert goes to Mrs. Brown's house.
In inverno Alberto va dalla signora Brown.

Mrs. Brown is an old friend of Timothy.
La signora Brown è una vecchia amica di Timoteo.
She lends Timothy her bathroom and, sometimes, her kitchen.
Presta a Timoteo la sua stanza da bagno e, qualche volta, la sua cucina.

Henry is Mr. Smith's son.
Enrico è il figlio del signor Smith.
Henry is very thin.
Enrico è molto magro.
He is an ice-cream seller.
Fa il venditore di gelati.
Sometimes he gives Timothy an ice-cream.
Qualche volta regala un gelato a Timoteo.

George is the keeper at the zoo.
Giorgio è il guardiano dello zoo.
George often gives Timothy a free ticket for the zoo.
Giorgio regala spesso a Timoteo un biglietto gratuito per lo zoo.
Timothy loves going to the zoo.
A Timoteo piace andare allo zoo.

Mr. Smith is a baker.
Il signor Smith fa il panettiere.
He is very fat.
È molto grasso.
He eats a lot of bread and cakes.
Mangia molto pane e molti dolci.
Sometimes he gives Timothy some cakes.
Qualche volta regala dei dolci a Timoteo.

Miss Miller is a teacher.
La signorina Miller fa l'insegnante.
She lends Timothy books.
Presta dei libri a Timoteo.
But Timothy can't read.
Ma Timoteo non sa leggere.
Miss Miller gives Timothy reading lessons.
La signorina Miller dà lezioni di lettura a Timoteo.

Mr. Scott is a farmer.
Il signor Scott fa l'agricoltore.
He has a barn and a lot of animals.
Ha un granaio e molti animali.
In winter, Timothy sleeps in the barn.
In inverno, Timoteo dorme nel granaio.

Professor Julian is interested in the stars.
Il professor Giuliano si occupa di stelle.
He looks at them all night long.
Le guarda tutta la notte.
He talks about the stars to Timothy.
Parla delle stelle a Timoteo.

Sylvia is an usherette at the cinema.
Silvia fa la maschera al cinema.
Sometimes she gives Timothy a free ticket.
Qualche volta regala a Timoteo un biglietto gratuito.

Peter is an astronaut.
Piero fa l'astronauta.
He talks about the moon to Timothy.
Parla della luna a Timoteo.
Timothy wants to go to the moon.
Timoteo vuole andare sulla luna.

Mrs. White is a taxi-driver.
La signora White fa l'autista di taxi.
Sometimes she gives Timothy a ride in her taxi.
Qualche volta fa fare un giro sul suo taxi a Timoteo.

Jeremy is a gipsy.
Geremia è uno zingaro.
He catches a lot of rabbits.
Cattura molti conigli.
He often gives Timothy a rabbit.
Spesso regala un coniglio a Timoteo.

Marion Scott is Mr. Scott's daughter.
Marianna Scott è la figlia del signor Scott.
She can't swim.
Non sa nuotare.
Timothy gives Marion swimming lessons.
Timoteo dà lezioni di nuoto a Marianna.

John loves watching football matches.
A Gianni piace guardare le partite di calcio.
Often Timothy goes with him.
Spesso Timoteo l'accompagna.

Bob is Timothy's faithful friend.
Bob è l'amico fedele di Timoteo.
He guards Timothy.
Fa la guardia a Timoteo.
But often, when he is on guard, Bob falls asleep.
Ma spesso, mentre monta la guardia, Bob si addormenta.

Timothy has a bath

Timothy loves having a bath.
Timoteo adora fare il bagno.

Timothy's toes
Le dita dei piedi di Timoteo

How many toes has he got?
Quante dita ha?

A red bath
Una vasca rossa

Timothy has washed up to here.
Timoteo si è lavato fino a qui.

A long brush
Una spazzola lunga

Soap
Sapone

Albert has walked here.
Di qui è passato Alberto.
Albert doesn't like washing.
Ad Alberto non piace lavarsi.

Who has walked here?
Chi è passato di qui?

They want to be...
Vorrebbero essere...

Mrs. Brown wants to be a ballet dancer.
La signora Brown vorrebbe essere una ballerina.

Mr. Smith wants first of all to be thin.
Il signor Smith vorrebbe innanzi tutto essere magro.

Then he wants to be a cowboy.
Poi vorrebbe essere un cowboy.

Bob wants to be a poodle.
Bob vorrebbe essere un barboncino.
He wants to win prizes in competitions.
Vorrebbe vincere premi ai concorsi.

Miss Miller wants to be a spy.
La signorina Miller vorrebbe essere una spia.
She wants to be beautiful and dangerous.
Vorrebbe essere bella e pericolosa.

Jeremy wants to be a pirate.
Geremia vorrebbe essere un pirata.
He wants to go in a ship to far-off countries.
Vorrebbe andare con la nave verso paesi lontani.

George wants to be a painter.
Giorgio vorrebbe essere un pittore.
He wants to paint portraits of all the animals in the zoo.
Vorrebbe fare il ritratto a tutti gli animali dello zoo.

Marion Scott wants to be a pop singer.
Marianna Scott vorrebbe essere una cantante pop.

Peter has had enough of the moon and the stars.
Piero ne ha abbastanza della luna e delle stelle.
He wants to be an under-water explorer.
Vorrebbe essere un esploratore subacqueo.

Professor Julian wants to be an astronaut.
Il professor Giuliano vorrebbe essere un astronauta.
He wants to be closer to the stars.
Vorrebbe essere più vicino alle stelle.

John wants to be a professional football player.
Gianni vorrebbe essere un giocatore di calcio professionista.
Or a disc-jockey.
Oppure un disc-jockey.

Mr. Scott likes money.
Al signor Scott piace il denaro.
He wants to be a millionaire.
Vorrebbe essere milionario.

Mrs. White has had enough of driving people in her taxi.
La signora White ne ha abbastanza di scarrozzare la gente sul suo taxi.
She wants to be rich.
Vorrebbe essere ricca.
She wants to take taxis herself.
Vorrebbe prendere lei il taxi.

Two giraffes
Due giraffe
One giraffe is called Genevieve.
Una giraffa si chiama Genoveffa.
The other one is called Alphonse.
L'altra si chiama Alfonso.

A tiger
Una tigre

Maurice is talking to the parrots.
Maurizio parla ai pappagalli.

Gorillas
Gorilla

A hippopotamus
Un ippopotamo

A bear
Un orso

An eagle
Un'aquila
He hates visitors.
Detesta i visitatori.

George, the keeper
Giorgio, il guardiano
He is talking to the monkeys.
Parla alle scimmie.
He understands them very well.
Le capisce benissimo.

At the zoo   *Allo zoo*

A lion and a lioness
Un leone e una leonessa
They are hungry.
Hanno fame.

Seals
Foche
They love diving.
Adorano tuffarsi.

A crocodile
Un coccodrillo

An elephant
Un elefante

A snake
Un serpente

The elephant's trunk
La proboscide dell'elefante

A flamingo
Un fenicottero

Mr. Smith is giving the penguins some cakes.
Il signor Smith dà dei dolci ai pinguini.

George and Genevieve
Giorgio e Genoveffa

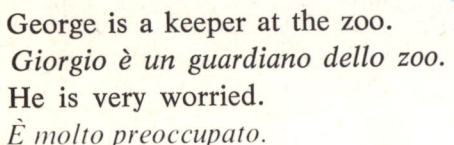

George is a keeper at the zoo.
Giorgio è un guardiano dello zoo.
He is very worried.
È molto preoccupato.

Genevieve, the giraffe, refuses to eat.
La giraffa Genoveffa si rifiuta di mangiare.
She is getting thin.
Sta dimagrendo.

George gives Genevieve some hay.
Giorgio dà a Genoveffa del fieno.
But she refuses to eat it.
Ma lei rifiuta di mangiarlo.

George gives Genevieve some green leaves.
Giorgio dà a Genoveffa delle foglie verdi.
She refuses to eat them.
Lei rifiuta di mangiarle.
She is getting thinner.
Dimagrisce sempre di più.

Genevieve is very, very thin.
Genoveffa è molto, molto magra.
The head of the zoo goes to see her.
Il direttore dello zoo va a farle visita.

« Go on, eat! » says the head to Genevieve.
« Avanti, mangia! » dice il direttore a Genoveffa.
But she refuses to eat.
Ma lei si rifiuta di mangiare.

Genevieve is free!
Genoveffa è libera!

She is very, very hungry.
Ha molta, molta fame.

She eats the leaves of the trees in the zoo.
Mangia le foglie degli alberi dello zoo.

George is in despair.
Giorgio è disperato.
Genevieve is going to die.
Genoveffa sta per morire.

But Genevieve doesn't die.
Ma Genoveffa non muore.
At night, she slips between the bars of her cage.
Durante la notte, scivola fra le sbarre della sua gabbia.

Genevieve escapes.
Genoveffa scappa.
Good-bye zoo!
Addio zoo!

Genevieve is very happy.
Genoveffa è felicissima.
But George and the head of the zoo are furious.
Ma Giorgio e il direttore dello zoo sono furibondi.

At the cinema   Al cinema

The cowboys wear white hats.
I cowboy portano il cappello bianco.
The gangsters wear black hats.
I fuorilegge portano il cappello nero.

A red velvet curtain
Una tenda di velluto rosso

An usherette
Una maschera
She is a friend of Sylvia.
È un'amica di Silvia.

She is selling chocolate and nuts.
Vende cioccolato e noccioline.
What else is she sellings?
Cos'altro vende?

The audience
Gli spettatori

Mrs. Scott
La signora Scott
She hates westerns.
Detesta i film western.
She is afraid of the gangsters.
Ha paura dei fuorilegge.

Mr. Scott and Marion
Il signor Scott e Marianna
They love westerns.
Adorano i western.

Where do they live?
Dove abitano?

The baby lives in a cot.
Il bambino vive in un lettino.
He hates his cot.
Detesta il suo lettino.

The Martians live on Mars.
I Marziani vivono su Marte.

Granny lives in a bungalow.
La nonna abita in una casetta.

The bear lives in the mountains.
L'orso vive sulle montagne.

The twins live in a sky-scraper.
I gemelli abitano in un grattacielo.
They are on the thirtieth floor.
Sono al trentesimo piano.

George lives in a tree-house.
Giorgio abita in una casetta sugli alberi.
It's not very strong.
Non è molto solida.

The mice live in a hole.
I topi vivono in una tana.
It's very dark.
È molto buia.

In winter, Timothy lives under a bridge.
In inverno Timoteo vive sotto un ponte.

The astronauts want to live on the moon.
Gli astronauti vorrebbero abitare sulla luna.

In summer, Timothy lives under a tree.
D'estate Timoteo vive sotto un albero.

The sailor lives on a ship.
Il marinaio vive su una nave.
Sometimes he is sea-sick.
Qualche volta ha il mal di mare.

The King lives in his castle.
Il re abita nel suo castello.
It's a bit cold there.
Ci fa un po' freddo.

The shepherd lives in a hut, with the lambs.
Il pastore abita in una capanna, insieme agli agnelli.

The monkey lives in the jungle.
La scimmia vive nella giungla.

The gipsy lives in a caravan.
Lo zingaro vive in un carrozzone.

Mr. Smith in the kitchen
Il signor Smith in cucina

Mr. Smith's cat
La gatta del signor Smith
She is very fat and very lazy.
È molto grassa e molto pigra.

Cakes
Dolci
Mr. Smith loves cakes.
Il signor Smith adora i dolci.

A cooker
Una cucina

A sink
Un lavandino

A washing-up machine
Una lavastoviglie
Mrs. Smith doesn't like washing up.
Alla signora Smith non piace lavare i piatti.

An oven
Un forno

An electric mixer
Un frullino elettrico

Mice
Topi

Recipe books
Libri di ricette

A table
Una tavola

How many books are there?
Quanti libri ci sono?

Timothy in hospital
Timoteo all'ospedale

Timothy is sick.
Timoteo è malato.
He is in hospital.
È all'ospedale.

Mrs. Brown visits Timothy.
La signora Brown fa visita a Timoteo.
She brings him some flowers.
Gli porta dei fiori.

George gives Timothy a book of tickets for the zoo.
Giorgio regala a Timoteo un blocchetto di biglietti per lo zoo.
Timothy loves going to the zoo.
A Timoteo piace molto andare allo zoo.

Jeremy the gipsy arrives.
Arriva Geremia, lo zingaro.
He brings some rabbit soup.
Gli porta del brodo di coniglio.
It's delicious!
È squisito!

Mr. Smith brings a huge box.
Il signor Smith porta una scatola enorme.
In the box there are six cakes.
Nella scatola ci sono sei dolci.

Miss Miller arrives.
Arriva la signorina Miller.
She brings some books.
Porta dei libri.
But Timothy can't read.
Ma Timoteo non sa leggere.

Sylvia gives Timothy a film magazine.
Silvia regala a Timoteo una rivista cinematografica.
In the magazine there are photos of film stars.
Nella rivista ci sono fotografie di stelle del cinema.

Henry Smith brings an ice-cream.
Enrico Smith porta un gelato.
Timothy has to eat the ice-cream very quickly!
Timoteo deve mangiare il gelato molto in fretta!

Timothy is surrounded by presents.
Timoteo è circondato di regali.
He doesn't feel sick any more.
Non si sente più malato.

Mrs. White arrives in her taxi.
La signora White arriva col suo taxi.
She doesn't bring any presents.
Non porta dei regali.
She takes Timothy away!
Porta via Timoteo!

From the helicopter
Dall'elicottero

The sun
Il sole

A cloud
Una nuvola

Birds
Uccelli

Cows
Mucche

A church
Una chiesa

Houses
Case

A roof
Un tetto

A bicycle
Una bicicletta

A car
Un'automobile

If I were a millionaire…
Se fossi un miliardario…

I would go round the world.
Farei il giro del mondo.

I would buy an island.
Comprerei un'isola.

I would eat twelve ice-creams every day.
Mangerei dodici gelati tutti i giorni.

I would buy a train and drive it.
Comprerei un treno e lo guiderei.

I would live in a forest with my friends.
Vivrei in una foresta con i miei amici.

I would have a house under the sea.
Avrei una casa sottomarina.

I would go to the moon.
Andrei sulla luna.

I would go to the circus every day.
Andrei al circo tutti i giorni.

I would buy a thousand balloons and I would fly.
Comprerei mille palloni e volerei.

I would live in a caravan...
Vivrei in un carrozzone...

...or perhaps in a modern caravan.
...oppure in una moderna roulotte.

Swimming *Il nuoto*

Timothy finds swimming exhausting.
Timoteo trova il nuoto faticosissimo.
Timothy loves strawberry ice-creams.
Timoteo adora i gelati alla fragola.
Red and orange are Timothy's favourite colours.
Il rosso e l'arancione sono i colori preferiti di Timoteo.

An ice-cream
Un gelato

Timothy loves cooking.
A Timoteo piace molto cucinare.
Timothy's kitchen
La cucina di Timoteo

Water-wings
Salvagente

Bathing trunks
Costume da bagno

A fish
Un pesce
The fish is eating the water-wings.
Il pesce sta mangiando il salvagente.

Timothy looks at television
Timoteo guarda la televisione

Timothy hasn't got television.
Timoteo non ha la televisione.
But he loves watching television.
Ma gli piace molto guardare la televisione.

Timothy goes into town.
Timoteo va in città.
He finds a television set.
Trova un televisore.

He watches a western.
Guarda un western.

He imitates the singers.
Imita i cantanti.

Then he watches a pop programme.
Poi guarda un programma pop.

He also imitates the comedians...
Imita anche i comici...

and he imitates the conductors...
e imita i direttori d'orchestra...

and he imitates the cooks...
e imita i cuochi...

and he imitates the sportsmen...
e imita gli sportivi...

and he imitates the dancers.
e imita i ballerini.

Timothy loves watching television.
A Timoteo piace molto guardare la televisione.
And people love watching Timothy!
E alla gente piace molto guardare Timoteo!

Paintings
Disegni
Which painting is the best?
Qual è il migliore disegno?

An Englishman eating fish and chips.
Un inglese che mangia fish-and-chips!

A map
Una carta geografica.

Flowers
Fiori

Stones
Pietre

Marion's green stone
La pietra verde di Marianna
She says it is
a precious stone.
*Lei dice che è
una pietra preziosa.*

Marion's mouse doesn't like television.
Al topo di Marianna non piace la televisione.

Books
Libri
How many books can you see in the classroom?
Quanti libri vedi nella classe?

An exercise book
Un quaderno

A rubber
Una gomma

A biro
Una biro

A ruler
Un righello

A pencil
Una matita

Chewing-gum
Gomma americana

Marion Scott at school
Marianna Scott a scuola

Miss Miller
La signorina Miller
She is a teacher.
È una maestra.

Marion Scott likes English lessons.
A Marianna Scott piacciono le lezioni d'inglese.
She likes watching television.
Le piace guardare la televisione.

Anne is afraid of mice.
Anna ha paura dei topi.
She is going to scream.
Sta per gridare.

Insects
Insetti

John likes television—but only when there is football on.
A Gianni piace la televisione, ma soltanto quando c'è la partita.
He is reading a football magazine.
Sta leggendo una rivista calcistica.

Who has walked this way?
Chi è passato di qui?

A fox
Una volpe

A woman in high heels
Una donna con i tacchi alti

A sledge
Una slitta

A dog
Un cane

A man with a stick
Un uomo con un bastone

A cat
Un gatto

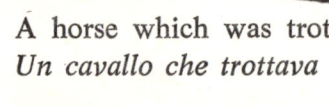
A horse which was trotting
Un cavallo che trottava

A horse which was galloping
Un cavallo che galoppava

A rabbit
Un coniglio

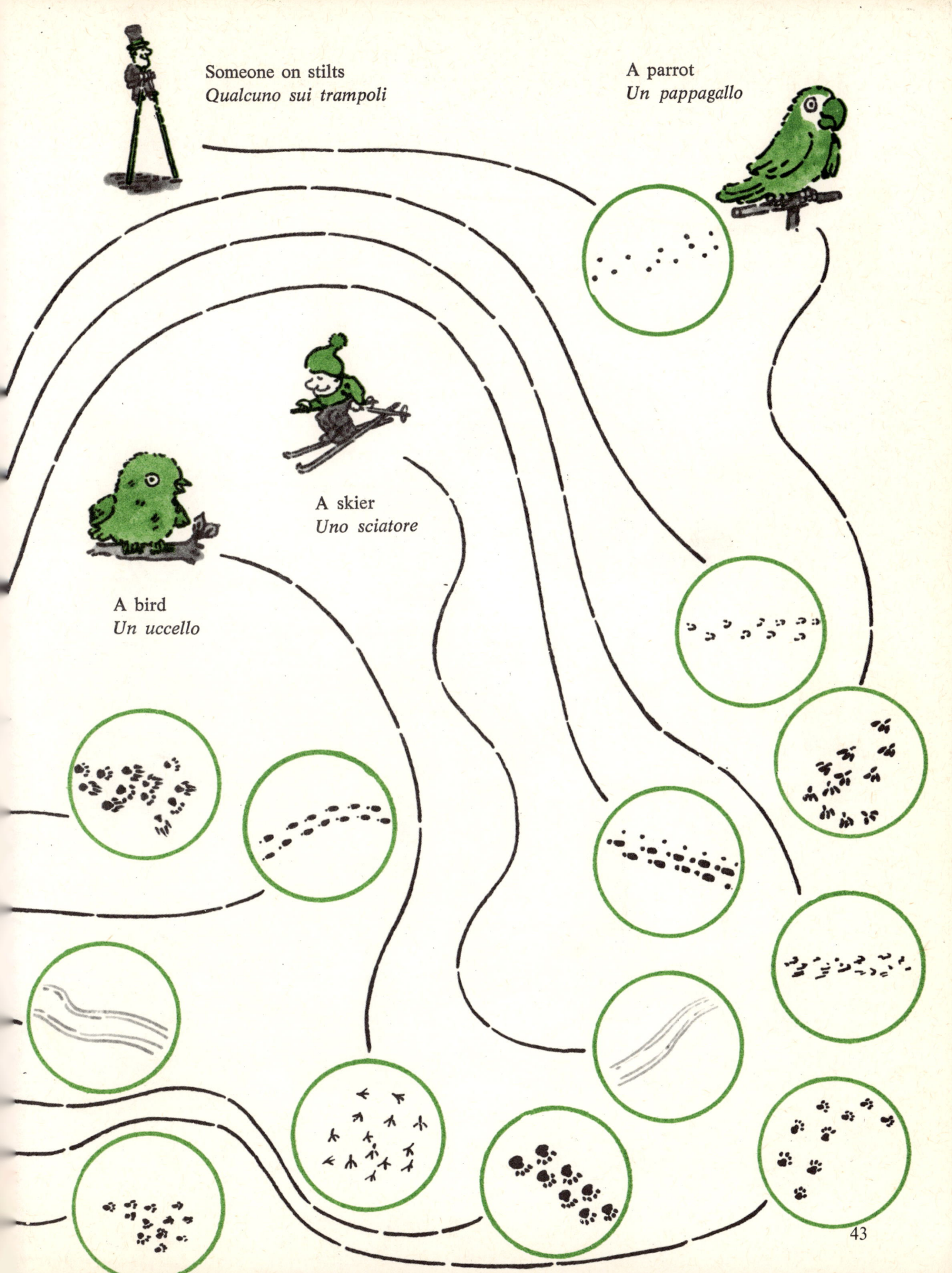

Jeremy the gipsy goes to bed
Geremia lo zingaro va a letto

Jeremy's coat is torn.
Il giaccone di Geremia è strappato.
He is mending it.
Lo sta rattoppando.

Jeremy is in his caravan.
Geremia è nel suo carrozzone.
Outside it is cold.
Fuori fa freddo.
Jeremy is warm.
Geremia ha caldo.

An alarm clock
Una sveglia
It doesn't work, but Jeremy likes it.
Non funziona, ma a Geremia piace.

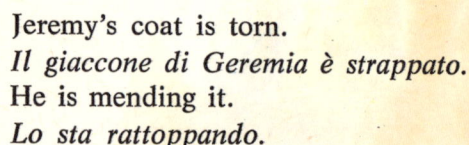

Jeremy's pyjamas
Il pigiama di Geremia

Jeremy's bed
Il letto di Geremia

Jeremy's dog
Il cane di Geremia.
He's called Flick.
Si chiama Flick.
He is looking at the sandwich.
Guarda il panino imbottito.

A sandwich
Un panino imbottito

A lucky horseshoe
Un ferro di cavallo porta-fortuna

A jersey
Una maglietta

A candle
Una candela

A television set
Un televisore
It doesn't work, but Jeremy likes it.
Non funziona, ma a Geremia piace.

Some cheese
Del formaggio

A mouse
Un topo

A waistcoat
Un panciotto
Jeremy found this waistcoat in the dustbin of a big hotel.
Geremia ha trovato questo panciotto nella pattumiera di un grande albergo.

Mrs. Brown's cake
La torta della signora Brown

Mrs. Brown is in her kitchen.
La signora Brown è nella sua cucina.
She is making a cake, with eggs, flour, butter and milk.
Sta preparando una torta con uova, farina, burro e latte.

Mrs. Brown puts the cake in the oven.
La signora Brown mette la torta in forno.
Albert looks at it.
Alberto la guarda.

When the cake is cooked, Mrs. Brown puts some cherries on it.
Quando la torta è cotta, la signora Brown ci mette sopra delle ciliege.

Mrs. Brown goes out of the kitchen.
La signora Brown esce dalla cucina.
Maurice the parrot comes in.
Entra Maurizio, il pappagallo.
He eats the cherries and flies away.
Mangia le ciliege e vola via.

Mrs. Brown comes back into the kitchen.
La signora Brown rientra in cucina.
How terrible!
Che orrore!
Who has eaten the cherries?
Chi ha mangiato le ciliege?
It must be Albert.
Dev'essere stato Alberto.

Maurice eats the cherry.
Maurizio mangia la ciliegia.

Mrs. Brown comes back.
La signora Brown ritorna.
On the cake she sees a mark: Maurice's claw.
Sulla torta vede un'impronta: l'artiglio di Maurizio.

Mrs. Brown covers the cake with chocolate.
La signora Brown ricopre la torta col cioccolato.
She puts one cherry in the middle.
Mette una ciliegia nel mezzo.
She takes Albert out of the kitchen.
Porta via Alberto dalla cucina.

Mrs. Brown takes a saucepan.
La signora Brown prende una pentola.
She's going to look for Maurice...
Va a cercare Maurizio...

A butterfly
Una farfalla

In the
In

A tree
Un albero

Some gnomes
Degli gnomi
Are they alive?
Sono vivi?

Leaves
Foglie

A swing
Un'altalena

A lawn
Un prato

A goldfish
Un pesce rosso
It is asleep.
Dorme.

A mole
Una talpa
It is asleep
Dorme

Roses
Rose

A mole-hill
Una montagnola fatta da una talpa.

Dew
Rugiada

48

garden early in the morning
giardino al mattino presto

The sun is rising.
Il sole sorge.

A hedge
Una siepe

A field-mouse
Un topo di campo
How many babies are there?
Quanti piccoli ci sono?

A bird
Un uccello
He is having his morning bath.
Fa il bagno mattutino.

Daffodils
Giunchiglie

Tulips
Tulipani

A caterpillar
Un bruco
How many caterpillars can you see?
Quanti bruchi vedi?

A squirrel
Uno scoiattolo
He is going to find some nuts.
Va a cercare delle noci.

Presents
Regali

A guinea pig
Un porcellino d'India

An astronaut costume
Una tuta da astronauta

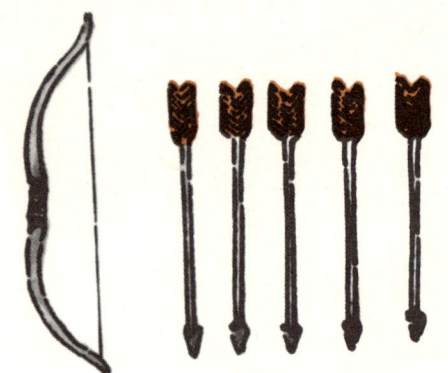
A bow and arrows
Un arco e delle frecce

A pot of paint
Un barattolo di vernice

Books
Libri

A camera
Una macchina fotografica
Who can you see in the photo?
Chi vedi nella foto?

Cards
Carte

Flower seeds
Semi di fiori

A money-box and some money
Un salvadanaio e del denaro

Masks
Maschere

A back-scratcher
Un raschietto

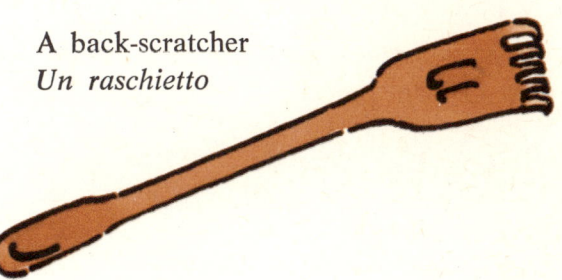

A puppet
Una marionetta

A puppy
Un cagnolino
Give him a name.
Dagli un nome.

A kite
Un aquilone

A canoe
Una canoa

A bicycle
Una bicicletta

A trampoline
Un telone

In the chocolate factory
Nella fabbrica di cioccolatini

Each kind of chocolate has a different decoration.
Ciascun tipo di cioccolatino ha una differente decorazione.

The decorating machine
La macchina per decorare

A scarf
Un foulard
All the operators have to wear a scarf.
Tutte le operaie devono portare un foulard.

This operator takes away faulty chocolates.
Quest'operaia toglie i cioccolatini difettosi.

The checker
L'addetta al controllo

A faulty chocolate
Un cioccolatino difettoso
Why is it faulty?
Perché è difettoso?

An operator
Un'operaia

She is Sylvia's sister—her twin.
È la sorella di Silvia: la sua gemella.

Timothy and John go to a football match
Timoteo e Gianni vanno alla partita

Timoteo and John love football.
Timoteo e Gianni adorano il calcio.
They are going to a match together.
Vanno alla partita insieme.

The *Lions* are playing the *Black Dogs*.
I Leoni giocano contro i Cani Neri.
Both teams are very strong.
Ambedue le squadre sono molto forti.

In the stadium there is an enormous crowd.
Nello stadio c'è una folla enorme.

Timothy and John shout to encourage the *Black Dogs*.
Timoteo e Gianni gridano per incoraggiare i Cani Neri.

The match begins.
La partita comincia.
The *Black Dogs* run very fast.
I Cani Neri corrono molto forte.
The captain of the *Black Dogs* is going to score a goal.
Il capitano dei Cani Neri sta per segnare una rete!

It's a goal!
È una rete!
But the ball doesn't stop.
Ma il pallone non si ferma.
It lands on Timothy's head!
Piomba sulla testa di Timoteo!
Timothy is dazed.
Timoteo è frastornato.

Timothy and John go to the exit.
Timoteo e Gianni vanno verso l'uscita.
The manager of the stadium arrives.
Arriva il direttore dello stadio.

He gives Timothy and John free tickets for the big match next week.
Regala a Timoteo e a Gianni dei biglietti gratuiti per la grande partita della prossima settimana.

Timothy and John are very pleased!
Timoteo e Gianni sono felicissimi!

Timothy at the seaside

Timothy doesn't like cold water.
A Timoteo non piace l'acqua fredda.

Bob likes swimming.
A Bob piace nuotare.

A sun umbrella
Un ombrellone
What colour is it?
Di che colore è?

A bikini
Un bikini

A dog
Un cane
He is looking for a bone.
Cerca un osso.

A spade
Una paletta

Sun-tan oil
Olio solare

Sun-glasses
Occhiali da sole

The baby is eating sand.
Il bambino mangia la sabbia.
He's eating pebbles too.
Mangia anche dei sassolini.

The baby's mother is asleep.
La madre del bambino dorme.
She wants to get sun-tanned.
Vuole abbronzarsi.
Is she sun-tanned?
È abbronzata?

Timoteo al mare

An ice-creamseller
Un gelataio

How many ice-creams can you see?
Quanti gelati vedi?

Marion Scott is learning to swim.
Marianna Scott impara a nuotare.

Bottles of Coca-cola
Bottiglie di Coca-cola

A bathing costume
Un costume da bagno

A paper hat
Un cappello di carta

This woman is looking at the dog.
Questa donna guarda il cane.

Shells
Conchiglie

A plastic dragon
Un drago di plastica

A rubber bone
Un osso di gomma

A bucket
Un secchiello

The children are making sand-castles.
I bambini fanno castelli di sabbia.

On holiday
In vacanza

At the sea-side
Al mare
Find a spade, a bucket and five shells.
Trova una paletta, un secchiello e cinque conchiglie.

On a canal
Sul canale
Would you like to live on a barge?
Ti piacerebbe vivere su un barcone?

In the mountains in winter
In montagna d'inverno
Who is ski-ing?
Chi sta sciando?
Do you know how to ski?
Sai sciare?

In the country
In campagna
Do you like picnics?
Ti piacciono i picnic?
What is the weather like?
Che tempo fa?

In the mountains in summer
In montagna d'estate
The sun is shining but there is still some snow.
Il sole brilla ma c'è ancora un po' di neve.

On a desert island
Su un'isola deserta
Are there any houses on the island?
Ci sono delle case sull'isola?

In the jungle
Nella giungla
It's raining.
Piove.
The parrots go under the trees.
I pappagalli vanno sotto gli alberi.

On a lake
Sul lago
Is it winter or summer?
È inverno o estate?

At the hairdresser's

Sylvia has very curly hair.
Silvia ha i capelli molto ricci.
She prefers straight hair.
Preferisce i capelli lisci.

Miss Jane is washing this woman's hair.
La signorina Gianna lava i capelli di questa signora.
The woman says that the water is too hot.
La signora dice che l'acqua è troppo calda.

Miss Miller doesn't like her hair.
Alla signorina Miller non piacciono i suoi capelli.
She wants to change it.
Li vuole cambiare.
She is choosing a wig.
Sceglie una parrucca.

Nail polish
Smalto per unghie

A comb
Un pettine

A hair-net
Una retina per capelli

Dal parrucchiere

Mrs. Brown is under the dryer.
La signora Brown è sotto il casco.
She is reading magazines.
Legge delle riviste.

How terrible!
Che orrore!
Mrs. White's hair has gone green!
I capelli della signora White sono diventati verdi!

Miss Anne is giving this woman a manicure.
La signorina Anna fa la manicure a questa signora.

A hair-brush
Una spazzola per capelli

Lacquer
Lacca

Rollers
Bigodini

Miss Miller buys a dog
La signorina Miller compra un cane

Miss Miller wants to buy a dog.
La signorina Miller vuole comprare un cane.

She goes to the pet-shop.
Va al negozio degli animali.

The shop is full of animals.
Il negozio è pieno di animali.

There are hamsters, guinea pigs, white mice, cats, canaries, rabbits and dogs.
Ci sono criceti, porcellini d'India, topolini bianchi, gatti, canarini, conigli e cani.

Miss Miller looks at the dogs.
La signorina Miller guarda i cani.

She chooses a small black dog.
Sceglie un piccolo cane nero.

The dog bites Miss Miller.
Il cane morde la signorina Miller.

Miss Miller doesn't want a dog any longer.
La signorina Miller non vuole più un cane.

Instead of a dog, she chooses four bowls of goldfish.
Invece di un cane, sceglie quattro vasi di pesci rossi.

Miss Miller is happy.
La signorina Miller è contenta.

Goldfish don't bite.
I pesci rossi non mordono.

The hockey match

The girls have scored four goals.
Le ragazze hanno segnato quattro reti.
The boys have scored only one goal.
I ragazzi hanno segnato una sola rete.

The spectators
Gli spettatori

They are all shouting "Hooray!"
Tutti gridano "Urrà!"
The boys are shouting less loudly than the girls.
I ragazzi gridano meno forte delle ragazze.

Lemons, for half-time
Limoni per l'intervallo

The referee
L'arbitro
He has been running a lot.
Ha corso molto.
What colour is his face?
Di che colore è il suo viso?

Shorts
Calzoncini

The captain of the girls' team
La capitana della squadra delle ragazze.
She is very pleased.
È molto contenta.

La partita di hockey

The ball has gone a long way away.
La palla è andata molto lontano.
Bob wants to find the ball.
Bob vuole trovare la palla.

The sports mistress of the girls' school is very pleased.
La professoressa di ginnastica delle ragazze è molto contenta.

She is very proud of her team.
È molto orgogliosa della sua squadra.

Is this a girl or a boy?
È una ragazza o un ragazzo?
How do you know?
Come lo sai?

A hockey stick
Una mazza da hockey

The captain of the boys' team
Il capitano della squadra dei ragazzi
He is furious.
È furibondo.
He is pretending to be pleased.
Finge di essere contento.

A sports shirt
Una maglia sportiva.

I'm going to be...
Diventerò...

A cook
Una cuoca

A reporter
Una giornalista

A model
Un'indossatrice

A housewife
Una casalinga

A pop singer
Una cantante pop

A doctor
Una dottoressa

A television interviewer
Un'intervistatrice televisiva

An air hostess
Una hostess di volo

A professional football player
Un calciatore professionista

An explorer
Un esploratore

A keeper at the zoo
Un guardiano dello zoo

An astronaut
Un astronauta

A jockey
Un fantino

A postman
Un postino

An actor
Un attore

A pilot
Un pilota

A mechanic
Un meccanico

A builder
Un muratore

The conductor
Il direttore d'orchestra
In his hand he has a white baton.
In mano ha una bacchetta bianca.
He is looking at the violinists with fury.
Guarda i violinisti furibondo.
They are playing badly.
Suonano male.

The first violinist
Il primo violino
He does not like the conductor.
A lui non piace il direttore d'orchestra.

The pianist
Il pianista

The male singer
Il cantante
He has a rather weak voice.
Ha una voce piuttosto debole.
He is afraid of the lady singer.
Ha paura della cantante.

A concert *Un concerto*

Drums
Tamburi

A French horn
Un corno francese

A double-bass
Un contrabbasso
The double-bass player is very small.
Il suonatore di contrabbasso è molto piccolo.
He can't see the conductor very well.
Non riesce a vedere bene il direttore d'orchestra.

Ear-rings
Orecchini

A diamond necklace
Una collana di diamanti
They are not real diamonds.
Non sono diamanti veri.

A red dress
Un vestito rosso

The lady singer
La cantante
She has a very powerful voice.
Ha una voce molto potente.

Gold shoes
Scarpe dorate

Timothy goes to the Motor Show
Timoteo va al Salone dell'Automobile

Timothy can't drive a car.
Timoteo non sa guidare l'automobile.

But he is interested in cars.
Però si interessa di automobili.

He decides to go to the Motor Show.
Decide di andare al Salone dell'Automobile.

But Timothy has no money.
Ma Timoteo non ha denaro.
He cannot pay the entrance fee.
Non può pagare l'ingresso.

But suddenly a man comes along.
Ma improvvisamente arriva un signore.

He shakes Timothy's hand.
Stringe la mano a Timoteo.

Timothy doesn't know why.
Timoteo non sa perché.

Timothy sees Mrs. White.
Timoteo vede la signora White.

They both get into the car.
Salgono tutti e due sull'automobile.

The man says: "You are the millionth visitor to the Motor Show!"
Il signore dice: « Lei è il milionesimo visitatore del Salone dell'Automobile! »

"You have won a prize!"
« Lei ha vinto un premio! »

The man shows Timothy his prize.
Il signore mostra a Timoteo il premio.
It is a huge car.
È un'enorme auto.

Timothy leaves the Motor Show.
Timoteo esce dal Salone dell'Automobile.

But he still hasn't paid the entrance fee!
E non ha ancora pagato il biglietto d'entrata!

In the playground
Al parco giochi

This boy doesn't like playing.
A questo bambino non piace giocare.
He prefers reading.
Preferisce leggere.
He's reading a sports magazine.
Legge una rivista sportiva.

Three girls are playing hopscotch.
Tre bambine giocano al gioco della settimana.

This girl has got a new skipping-rope.
Questa bambina ha una nuova corda per saltare.
She can do three hundred skips without stopping.
Sa fare trecento salti senza fermarsi.

This girl is doing her homework.
Questa bambina fa i compiti.

Marion Scott is putting on her roller skates.
Marianna Scott si mette i pattini a rotelle.

These girls are playing hide and seek.
Queste bambine giocano a nascondino.
Find the girl who is hiding.
Trova la bambina che si è nascosta.

This boy is smoking a cigarette.
Questo ragazzino fuma una sigaretta.
What colour is his face?
Di che colore è il suo viso?

John is playing football with his pals.
Gianni gioca a pallone con i suoi compagni.

These two boys are hungry.
Questi due ragazzi hanno fame.
What are they eating?
Cosa mangiano?

Parents and children
Genitori e bambini

Henry Smith is thin.
Enrico Smith è magro.
His father, Mr. Smith, is fat.
Suo padre, il signor Smith, è grasso.
His mother, Mrs. Smith, is neither fat nor thin.
Sua madre, la signora Smith, non è né grassa né magra.

Here are four worms: grandfather, father, son and grandson.
Ecco quattro vermi: nonno, padre, figlio e nipote.
Which is the father?
Qual è il padre?

This giant is very tall.
Questo gigante è molto alto.
His daughter is very short.
Sua figlia è molto piccola.
She is a baby.
È una bimba.

This kangaroo has its child in its pouch.
Questo canguro ha il suo piccolo nel marsupio.

This lamb has no mother.
Questo agnellino non ha mamma.
The shepherd gives it some milk.
Il pastore gli dà del latte.

This puppy's mother is a poodle.
La madre di questo cucciolo è una barboncina.
His father is a boxer.
Suo padre è un boxer.
The puppy is neither a poodle nor a boxer.
Il cucciolo non è né un barboncino, né un boxer.

Here are a man, his wife, his son, his daughter and his dog.
Ecco un signore, sua moglie, suo figlio, sua figlia, il suo cane.
They look like one another.
Si assomigliano l'uno con l'altro.

Peter goes to the moon
Piero va sulla luna

A photo of Peter's girl-friend
Una foto della ragazza di Piero

A photo of Peter's father and mother
Una foto del padre e della madre di Piero

A photo of the inventor of the spacecraft
Una foto dell'inventore della nave spaziale

Peter's tea
La merenda di Piero

Peter's lunch
Il pranzo di Piero

Peter's breakfast
La colazione di Piero

The sky is dark blue.
Il cielo è blu scuro.

Stars
Stelle

Professor Julian is looking at the spacecraft through his telescope.
Il professor Giuliano guarda la nave spaziale con il suo telescopio.
He would love to go to the moon.
Gli piacerebbe molto andare sulla luna.

Mrs. Brown chooses a hat
La signora Brown sceglie un cappello

Mrs. Brown wants to buy herself a new hat.
La signora Brown vuole comprarsi un cappello nuovo.
There is a big choice.
C'è molta scelta.

She tries on a big hat.
Prova un cappello grande.

Next she puts on a small hat.
Poi si mette un cappellino.

Mrs. Brown loves black.
La signora Brown adora il nero.
She puts on a black hat with a veil.
Si mette un cappello nero con una veletta.

The salesgirl chooses a hat covered in flowers.
La commessa sceglie un cappello ornato di fiori.
Mrs. Brown doesn't like it.
Alla signora Brown non piace.

Mrs. Brown tries on a plastic hat.
La signora Brown prova un cappello di plastica.
It doesn't suit her.
Non le va bene.

Mrs. Brown can't find a hat.
La signora Brown non trova un cappello.

Suddenly, Mrs. Brown notices a hat with feathers.
Improvvisamente la signora Brown nota un cappello con le piume.
It's perfect!
È perfetto!

But it's another woman's hat.
Però è il cappello di un'altra signora.

Mrs. Brown gives the woman some money.
La signora Brown dà alla donna del denaro.
Both of them are very pleased.
Tutte e due sono molto contente.

At the

Timothy is trying to put on some skates.
Timoteo cerca di mettersi i pattini.
He doesn't want to skate.
Non vuole pattinare.
He is afraid of falling down.
Ha paura di cadere.

The snack bar
Il bar

Albert likes watching the skaters.
Ad Alberto piace guardare i pattinatori.

Mr. Smith is too fat to skate.
Il signor Smith è troppo grasso per pattinare.
He skates because he wants to get thin.
Pattina perché vuole dimagrire.

White boots
Stivaletti bianchi

Miss Miller doesn't skate very well.
La signorina Miller non pattina molto bene.
She is trying to learn from a book.
Cerca di imparare da un libro.

Sylvia skates very badly.
Silvia pattina molto male.
But she has a lot of friends.
Ma ha molti amici.
They help her.
L'aiutano.

ice-rink Sulla pista di pattinaggio

Mr. Scott is watching Marion.
Il signor Scott guarda Marianna.
He is very proud of her.
È molto orgoglioso di lei.

A short skirt
Una gonna corta

This lady is Russian.
Questa signora è russa.
She learned to skate when she was two years old.
Ha imparato a pattinare quando aveva due anni.

Marion Scott skates very well.
Marianna Scott pattina molto bene.
She can dance.
Sa ballare.
It is difficult to watch Marion.
È difficile guardare Marianna.

Skates
Pattini

The skating teacher
L'istruttore di pattinaggio
He is very conceited.
È molto vanitoso.

Skeletons
Scheletri

Find the drawing which goes with each skeleton.
Trova l'immagine che corrisponde a ciascuno scheletro.

A dinosaur
Un dinosauro

There are no more dinosaurs.
Di dinosauri non ce ne sono più.

A gorilla
Un gorilla
Its skeleton looks like the next skeleton.
Il suo scheletro assomiglia a quello seguente.

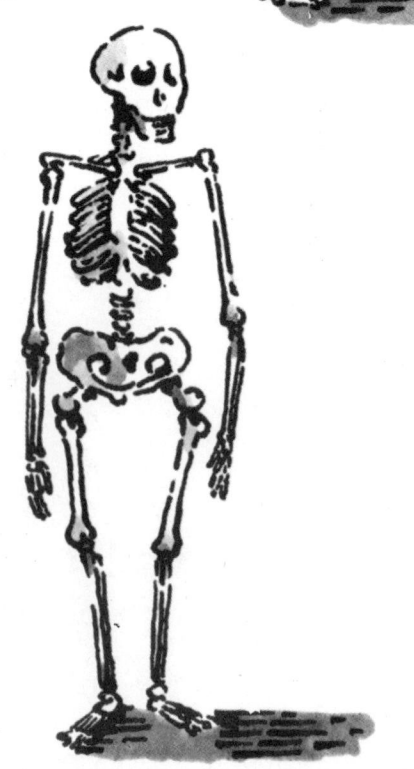

A man
Un uomo
How many bones can you see?
Quante ossa vedi?

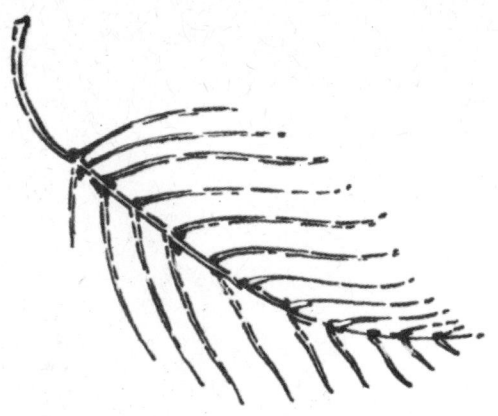

A leaf
Una foglia
Here are the veins of a leaf.
Ecco le venature di una foglia.

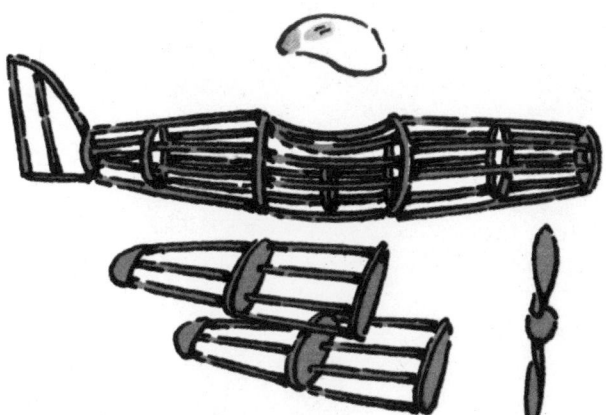

An aeroplane
Un aeroplano
This is a model.
Questo è un modellino.

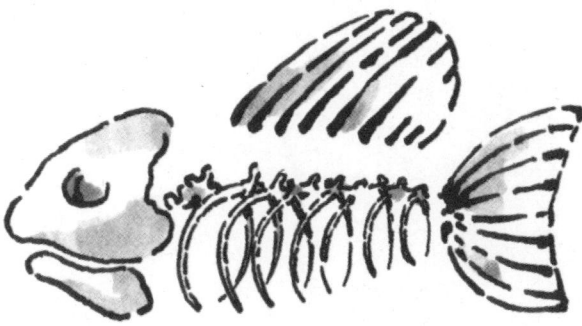

A fish
Un pesce
I think it's a herring.
Penso sia un'aringa.

On the escalator

Jeremy, the gipsy
Geremia, lo zingaro
What has he got under his arm?
Cos'ha sotto il braccio?

Timothy is looking at the advertisements.
Timoteo guarda i cartelloni pubblicitari.
He sees a picture of a big bed.
Vede l'immagine di un grande letto.
Timothy has no bed.
Timoteo non ha letto.

Albert doesn't like the escalator.
Ad Alberto non piace la scala mobile.

Maurice doesn't need a staircase.
Maurizio non ha bisogno della scala.
He flies above everybody.
Vola sopra a tutti.

A fur coat
Una pelliccia

A shopping basket
Una borsa per la spesa

An umbrella
Un ombrello

This woman is very surprised to see a parrot.
Questa signora è molto stupita di vedere un pappagallo.

Sulla scala mobile

John is trying to go down the up staircase.
Gianni cerca di scendere la scala che sale.

A grandmother
Una nonna
She hates the escalator.
Detesta la scala mobile.
It goes too fast.
Va troppo veloce.

Gloves
Guanti

A grandfather
Un nonno
He is trying to help his wife.
Cerca di aiutare sua moglie.

A bowler hat
Una bombetta

A handbag
Una borsetta

A large suitcase
Una grossa valigia

An overcoat
Un soprabito

Somebody is trying to help the grandfather.
Qualcuno cerca di aiutare il nonno.

Mrs. Brown and Timothy make bread
La signora Brown e Timoteo fanno il pane

Mrs. Brown and Timothy are making bread.
La Signora Brown e Timoteo stanno facendo il pane.
They mix together flour, water and salt.
Impastano la farina con acqua e sale.

Timothy tries to read the recipe.
Timoteo cerca di leggere la ricetta.
Mrs. Brown puts in two spoonfuls of yeast.
La signora Brown aggiunge due cucchiai di lievito.

They put the bread on the radiator.
Mettono il pane sul calorifero.

The bread will become twice as big.
Il pane diventerà grande il doppio.

Mrs. Brown and Timothy go out of the kitchen.
La signora Brown e Timoteo escono dalla cucina.
The bread begins to get bigger.
Il pane comincia a diventare più grosso.

An hour later Mrs. Brown and Timothy come back.
Un'ora dopo la signora Brown e Timoteo ritornano.

The bread has overflowed!
Il pane è traboccato!

The radiator is covered in bread.
Il calorifero è ricoperto di pane.

Mrs. Brown looks at the recipe.
La signora Brown guarda la ricetta.

There was too much yeast in the bread.
C'era troppo lievito nel pane.

It's Timothy's fault.
È colpa di Timoteo.

Mrs. Brown takes a bit of the bread.
La signora Brown prende un pezzo di pane.
She eats it.
Lo mangia.

The bread is cooked.
Il pane è cotto.
All's well that ends well.
Tutto è bene quel che finisce bene.
Timothy and Mrs. Brown have a delicious supper.
Timoteo e la signora Brown fanno una cenetta squisita.

They don't sit at the table.
Non si mettono a tavola.

They eat off the radiator!
Mangiano direttamente dal calorifero!

My family
La mia famiglia

One of my cousins
Uno dei miei cugini
He's called Paul.
Si chiama Paolo.
He's sailor.
È un marinaio.

One of my aunts
Una mia zia
A guinea pig has just bitten her.
Un porcellino d'India l'ha appena morsa.

My grandmother
Mia nonna
She has blue hair.
Ha i capelli azzurri.

My father
Mio padre
His shirt is too tight.
La sua camicia è troppo stretta.

My grandfather
Mio nonno

Me!
Io!

Four little cousins
Quattro cuginetti

My uncle
Mio zio
He is my father's brother.
È il fratello di mio padre.
They are twins.
Sono gemelli.

Another uncle
Un altro zio
He's my favourite aunt's husband.
È il marito della mia zia preferita.

My sister
Mia sorella
She loves making herself up.
Le piace molto truccarsi.

My godfather
Il mio padrino

My favourite aunt
La mia zia preferita

My brother
Mio fratello

My mother
Mia madre
She is trying to smile.
Cerca di sorridere.

Claude is my godfather's dog.
Claudio è il cane del mio padrino.

He is nine, and he has three guinea pigs.
Ha nove anni e tre porcellini d'India.

I like eating...
Mi piace mangiare...

I like eating vegetables.
Mi piace mangiare la verdura.

I particularly like:
Mi piacciono soprattutto:

Peas
Piselli

Carrots
Carote

Potatoes (especially chips)
Patate (specialmente fritte)

Lettuce
Lattuga

Cucumbers
Cetrioli

Brussels sprouts
Cavolini di Bruxelles

But I don't like:
Ma non mi piacciono:

Spinach
Spinaci

Onions
Cipolle

I like eating fruit.
Mi piace mangiare la frutta.

My favourite fruits are:
I frutti che preferisco sono:

Pineapples **Pears**
Ananas *Pere*

Grapefruit (and grapefruit juice)
Pompelmo (e succo di pompelmo)

Bananas **Peaches** **Melons**
Banane *Pesche* *Meloni*

Strawberries (and strawberry ice-cream)
Fragole (e gelato alla fragola)

Apricots (particularly apricot yogurt)
Albicocche (specialmente lo yogurt all'albicocca)

Plums **Apples**
Prugne *Mele*

I like eating all fruits—except lemons.
Mi piace mangiare tutta la frutta—eccetto i limoni.

I like bread, with lots of butter and jam.
Mi piace il pane con molto burro e marmellata.

I like biscuits and cakes.
Mi piacciono i biscotti e i dolci.

I don't like eggs much.
Non mi piacciono molto le uova.
I love meat, especially hamburgers.
Mi piace molto la carne, soprattutto gli hamburger.

I like drinking Coca-cola or tea.
Mi piace bere la Coca-cola o il tè.
I hate milk.
Detesto il latte.

My favourite dish is spaghetti with tomato sauce and cheese and a sausage.
Il mio piatto preferito è: spaghetti con salsa di pomodoro, formaggio e salsiccia.

Henry Smith admires Peter.
Enrico Smith ammira Piero.
He wants to be an astronaut too.
Anche lui vuole essere un astronauta.

Peter the
Il compleanno

Peter is looking at his birthday cake.
Piero guarda la sua torta di compleanno.

Mrs. Brown
La signora Brown
She made the cake yesterday.
Ha fatto la torta ieri.
She is very proud of it.
Ne è molto orgogliosa.

Candles
Candeline

Peter's birthday cake
La torta di compleanno di Piero
It is in the shape of the moon.
Ha la forma della luna.

Lemonade
Limonata

A glass
Un bicchiere

Tomato sandwiches
Tramezzini al pomodoro

The table-cloth
La tovaglia

A cup
Una tazza

A knife
Un coltello

Who is under the table?
Chi c'è sotto la tavola?

astronaut's birthday
di Piero l'astronauta

Mrs. White
La signora White
She is a friend of Peter.
È un'amica di Piero.
When he comes back from the moon, she always collects him in her taxi.
Quando ritorna dalla luna, lo carica sempre sul suo taxi.

Timothy loves birthdays.
A Timoteo piacciono molto i compleanni.
He particularly loves peanuts.
Gli piacciono specialmente le noccioline.

Peanuts
Noccioline

A spoon
Un cucchiaio

Strawberry ice-cream
Gelato alla fragola

Ham sandwiches
Tramezzini al prosciutto

Henry Smith brought two large bowls of ice-cream.
Enrico Smith ha portato due grosse coppe di gelato.

A tie
Una cravatta
It's a present from Professor Julian.
È un regalo del professor Giuliano.
How many stars can you see?
Quante stelle vedi?

Jeremy goes to the races
Geremia va alle corse

Jeremy is cold and hungry.
Geremia ha freddo e fame.

He wants to buy himself a blanket and some cheese.
Vuole comprarsi una coperta e del formaggio.

But he has no money.
Ma non ha denaro.

But he has a lot of heather.
Però ha molta erica.
He makes it into lots of small sprigs.
Ne fa tanti mazzolini.

He goes to the races.
Va alle corse.
At the track there are a lot of people.
Lungo la pista c'è molta gente.

Jeremy sells a few sprigs of heather.
Geremia vende qualche mazzolino di erica.
People think that heather is lucky.
La gente crede che l'erica porti fortuna.

A fat man buys four sprigs.
Un uomo grasso ne compra quattro mazzetti.

His horse is going to run in the next race.
Il suo cavallo correrà nella corsa successiva.

He needs good luck.
Ha bisogno di fortuna.

Suddenly, the fat man comes back.
Improvvisamente l'uomo grasso ritorna.
His horse has won!
Il suo cavallo ha vinto!

The fat man is very happy.
L'uomo grasso è molto contento.
He buys all Jeremy's heather.
Compra tutta l'erica di Geremia.

But in two hours Jeremy has sold only ten sprigs.
Ma in due ore Geremia ha venduto solo dieci mazzolini.

Jeremy is very happy too.
Anche Geremia è molto contento.

He has enough money to buy himself two blankets, some cheese, a box of chocolates and a cigar!
Ha abbastanza denaro da comprarsi due coperte, del formaggio, una scatola di cioccolatini e un sigaro!

Seagulls
Gabbiani

Clouds
Nuvole

John is looking out of the window.
Gianni guarda dalla finestra.
He loves the movement of the hovercraft.
Gli piace molto il movimento dell'aliscafo.
He is very happy.
È molto contento.

It is raining.
Piove.

The hostess
La hostess
She prefers travelling by plane.
Preferisce viaggiare in aereo.

The sea-water is salty.
L'acqua del mare è salata.

Waves
Onde

Timothy in a hovercraft
Timoteo in aliscafo

The captain of the hovercraft
Il comandante dell'aliscafo

Timothy is looking out of the window.
Timoteo guarda fuori dal finestrino.
What colour is Timothy's face?
Di che colore è il viso di Timoteo?
He is feeling sea-sick.
Ha il mal di mare.

Bob is feeling sea-sick too.
Anche Bob ha il mal di mare.

A fish
Un pesce

The hovercraft
L'aliscafo
It does not touch the water.
Non tocca l'acqua.
It is on a cushion of air.
È su un cuscino d'aria.

How many fish can you see?
Quanti pesci vedi?

House for sale
Casa in vendita

This house is for sale.
Questa casa è in vendita.

People are looking at it.
Delle persone la guardano.

Is the house finished?
È finita la casa?

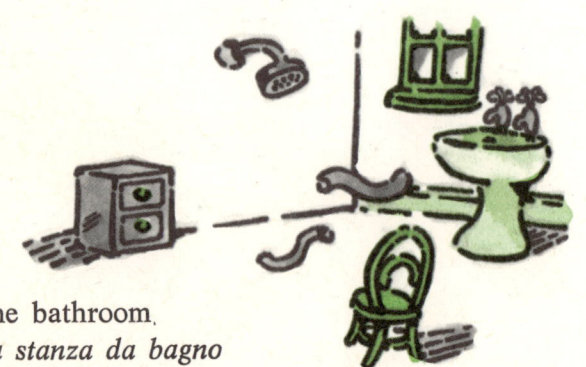

The bathroom
La stanza da bagno
Where is the bath?
Dov'è la vasca da bagno?

The kitchen
La cucina
Where is the sink?
Dov'è il lavandino?

The refrigerator
Il frigorifero

A bedroom
Una camera da letto

How many beds are there?
Quanti letti ci sono?

The dining-room
La sala da pranzo

The staircase
La scala

The builders and painters are hungry.
I muratori e gli imbianchini hanno fame.

The hall
L'ingresso

The living-room
Il soggiorno

A chair
Una sedia

A sofa
Un divano

An armchair
Una poltrona

The garden
Il giardino

A bulldozer
Una scavatrice

In an office
In un ufficio

The boss
Il capo
He is rich.
È ricco.
He wants to be even richer.
Vuole essere ancora più ricco.

A painting of the boss
Un ritratto del capo
Does it look like the boss?
Assomiglia al capo?

A cigar
Un sigaro

The boss's secretary
La segretaria del capo

She is answering both the telephones.
Risponde a tutt'e due i telefoni.

She is talking to New York and to Milan at the same time.
Parla contemporaneamente con New York e con Milano.

But she cannot speak Italian.
Ma non parla italiano.

So she is not saying much to Milan.
Così non parla molto con Milano.

Big buildings
Grandi edifici

A factory
Una fabbrica
Everybody is working.
Tutti lavorano.

A school
Una scuola
Nearly everyone is working.
Quasi tutti lavorano.

An office block
Un palazzo di uffici

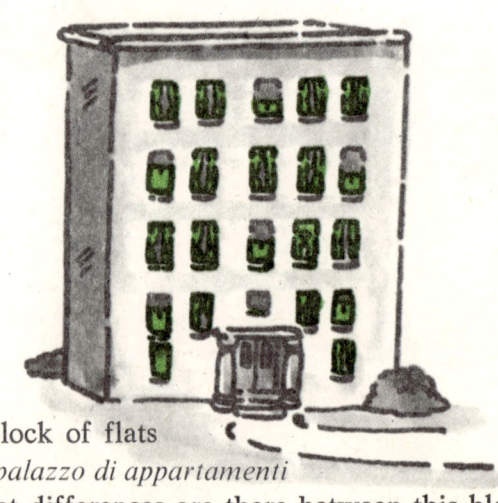

A block of flats
Un palazzo di appartamenti
What differences are there between this block and the office block?
Che differenza c'è tra questo palazzo e quello per uffici?

A library
Una biblioteca
There are books everywhere.
Ci sono libri dappertutto.

A cathedral
Una cattedrale
It is very old.
È molto antica.

A department store
Un grande magazzino
In this store you can buy everything you want.
In questo magazzino puoi comprare tutto ciò che vuoi.

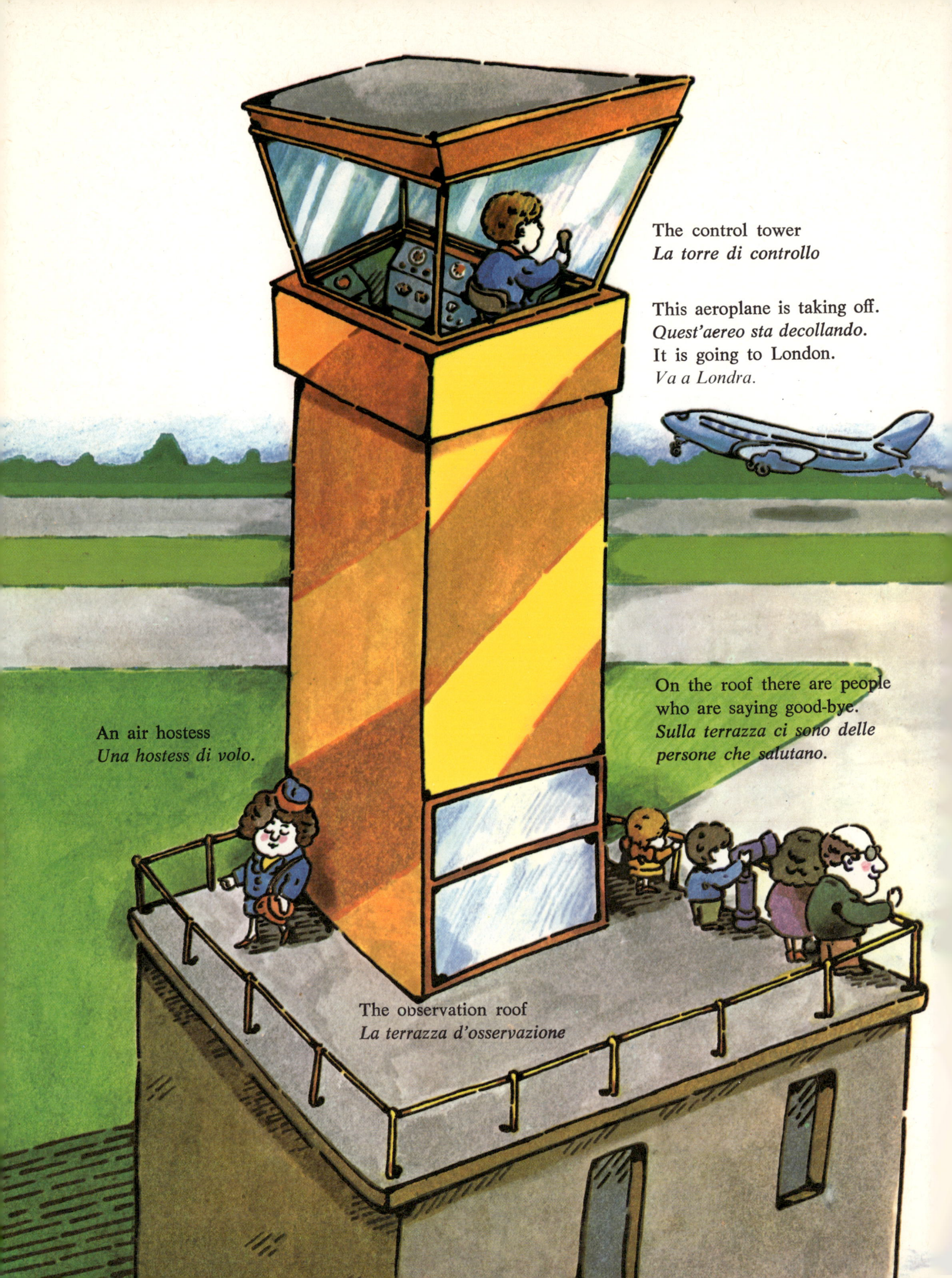

The control tower
La torre di controllo

This aeroplane is taking off.
Quest'aereo sta decollando.
It is going to London.
Va a Londra.

On the roof there are people who are saying good-bye.
Sulla terrazza ci sono delle persone che salutano.

An air hostess
Una hostess di volo.

The observation roof
La terrazza d'osservazione

At the airport
All'aeroporto

This aeroplane is landing.
Quest'aereo atterra.
One of its engines has broken down.
Uno dei motori si è guastato.

Ambulances are waiting.
Le autoambulanze stanno aspettando.

An airport bus
Un autobus dell'aeroporto
It goes to the town terminal.
Va al terminal in città.

Luggage
Bagagli

A pilot
Un pilota

A jet plane
Un aereo a reazione

A fire engine
Un'auto dei pompieri

The burglars
I ladri

It's winter.
È inverno.
Timothy and Bob are looking for a warm place to spend the night.
Timoteo e Bob cercano un posto caldo per passare la notte.

In the street there are also two burglars.
Per la strada ci sono anche due ladri.
The burglars go to Mr. and Mrs. Fisher's house.
I ladri vanno a casa dei signori Fisher.

They break the lock on the door.
Forzano la serratura della porta.
The burglars fill their sacks.
I ladri riempiono i loro sacchi.

Suddenly they hear a noise.
Improvvisamente sentono un rumore.
Jane Fisher walks in her sleep.
Gianna Fisher è sonnambula.

Mr. and Mrs. Fisher wake up.
Il signore e la signora Fisher si svegliano.
Mr. Fisher telephones the police.
I signori Fisher si svegliano.

They think she is a ghost.
Credono che sia un fantasma.
They run away.
Scappano.

The policeman takes the burglars away.
Il poliziotto porta via i ladri.

Mr. and Mrs. Fisher thank Timothy.
I signori Fisher ringraziano Timoteo.

Timothy and Bob are there.
Timoteo e Bob sono lì.
They are trying to get warm.
Stanno cercando di riscaldarsi.
Timothy grabs the burglars and Bob barks.
Timoteo acchiappa i ladri e Bob abbaia.

They give him a warm and comfortable bed.
Gli danno un letto caldo e confortevole.
Timothy and Bob are very happy.
Timoteo e Bob sono molto felici.

At the wax museum

Al museo delle cere

Queen Elizabeth I of England
La regina Elisabetta I d'Inghilterra
She often wore pearls in her hair.
Portava spesso delle perle nei capelli.

A nineteenth-century explorer
Un esploratore del diciannovesimo secolo

Mohammad Ali, the boxing champion
Mohammed Alì, il campione di pugilato

A footballer
Un calciatore

John is looking at the footballer.
Gianni guarda il calciatore.
He wants to be a professional footballer.
Vorrebbe fare il calciatore di professione.

Red Indians
Pellerossa

How do they get around?
Come viaggiano

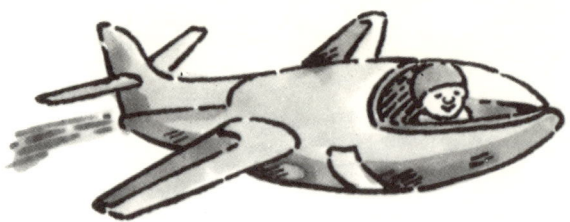

The pilot flies in a jet plane.
Il pilota vola su un aereo a reazione.

Jeremy gets around in his caravan.
Geremia viaggia con il suo carrozzone.
His horse goes very slowly.
Il suo cavallo cammina molto lentamente.
When he's hungry, the horse stops.
Quando ha fame, il cavallo si ferma.

Bob walks.
Bob cammina.
When he is very tired Timothy carries him.
Quando è molto stanco, Timoteo lo porta in braccio.

Peter gets around in a spacecraft.
Piero viaggia su una nave spaziale.

Maurice flies.
Maurizio vola.
He goes very fast.
Va molto veloce.
He never has problems with the traffic.
Non ha mai problemi di traffico.

Timothy gets around on foot.
Timoteo viaggia a piedi.
He doesn't go very quickly.
Non va molto veloce.

Mrs. White gets around in her taxi.
La signora White viaggia con il suo taxi.
She likes going fast.
Le piace andare forte.
When the traffic is bad she is furious.
Quando il traffico è intenso è furibonda.

The bus driver gets around in a bus.
Il conducente dell'autobus viaggia in autobus.

The millionaire gets around in a big yacht.
Il miliardario viaggia su un grande panfilo.

Miss Miller doesn't like going fast.
La signorina Miller non ama andare veloce.
She gets around on a bicycle.
Viaggia in bicicletta.

Marion Scott has got some roller skates.
Marianna Scott ha dei pattini a rotelle.
Her white mice love going fast.
Ai suoi topolini bianchi piace andare forte.

And you?
E tu?

How do you get around?
Voi, come viaggi?

At the Scotts' house in the evening

Mr. Scott is looking at the television.
Il signor Scott guarda la televisione.

He loves sports programmes.
Adora i programmi sportivi.

Rubber boots
Stivali di gomma

How many pairs are there?
Quante paia ce ne sono?

Mr. Scott's dog
Il cane del signor Scott

A lamb
Un agnellino

La sera in casa Scott

A lamp
Una lampada

Marion always sucks her biro.
Marianna succhia sempre la sua biro.

Mrs. Scott is making a dress.
La signora Scott sta facendo un vestito.

Cotton
Filo

A biro
Una biro

A sewing machine
Una macchina da cucire

Marion's pencil-sharpener
Il tempera-matite di Marianna

The material
Il tessuto

It is shaped like a whale.
Ha la forma di una balena.

The pattern
Il modello

Marion Scott is doing her homework.
Marianna Scott sta facendo i compiti.

She hates maths.
Detesta la matematica.

She loves dresses with flowers.
Le piacciono molto i vestiti a fiori.

Miss Miller nearly always gives her nought.
La signorina Miller le dà quasi sempre zero.

How many flowers can you see?
Quanti fiori vedi?

Does Mrs. Scott look like the woman in the pattern?
La signora Scott somiglia alla donna del figurino?

It has no mother.
Non ha mamma.

Do you know?
Lo sai?

The months of the year	I mesi dell'anno
January	gennaio
February	febbraio
March	marzo
April	aprile
May	maggio
June	giugno
July	luglio
August	agosto
September	settembre
October	ottobre
November	novembre
December	dicembre

The seasons of the year	Le stagioni dell'anno
spring	primavera
summer	estate
autumn	autunno
winter	inverno

The days of the week	I giorni della settimana
Monday	lunedì
Tuesday	martedì
Wednesday	mercoledì
Thursday	giovedì
Friday	venerdì
Saturday	sabato
Sunday	domenica

The compass	La bussola
North	Nord
South	Sud
East	Est
West	Ovest

Travelling	In viaggio
the road	la strada
a main road	la strada principale
the motorway	l'autostrada
closed to traffic	chiuso al traffico
no waiting	divieto di sosta
lorries	autocarri
keep right	tenere la destra
move along	circolare
look out	attenzione
a parking ticket	una multa
traffic police	vigili
a policeman on a motorbike	un poliziotto in motocicletta
help!	aiuto!
I am so sorry	mi spiace molto
sorry	scusi
excuse me	scusi

The continents / *I continenti*

Africa	*Africa*
Asia	*Asia*
Australasia	*Oceania*
Europe	*Europa*
North America	*Nord America*
South America	*Sud America*

Some countries / *Alcuni paesi*

Australia	*Australia*
Austria	*Austria*
Argentina	*Argentina*
Belgium	*Belgio*
Canada	*Canada*
Denmark	*Danimarca*
England	*Inghilterra*
Eire	*Irlanda*
Finland	*Finlandia*
France	*Francia*
Germany	*Germania*
Greece	*Grecia*
Holland	*Olanda*
Hungary	*Ungheria*
Italy	*Italia*
Mexico	*Messico*
Luxemburg	*Lussemburgo*
Northern Ireland	*Irlanda del Nord*
Norway	*Norvegia*
New Zealand	*Nuova Zelanda*
Poland	*Polonia*
Portugal	*Portogallo*
Russia	*Russia*
Scotland	*Scozia*
South Africa	*Sud Africa*
Spain	*Spagna*
Sweden	*Svezia*
Switzerland	*Svizzera*
Turkey	*Turchia*
United States of America	*Stati Uniti d'America*
Wales	*Galles*
Yugoslavia	*Jugoslavia*

Some colours / *Alcuni colori*

red	*rosso*
blue	*blu*
green	*verde*
yellow	*giallo*
white	*bianco*
black	*nero*
violet	*viola*
brown	*marrone*
dark brown	*bruno*
pink	*rosa*
orange	*arancio*
maroon	*amaranto*

Some numbers / *Alcuni numeri*

one	*uno*
two	*due*
three	*tre*
four	*quattro*
five	*cinque*
six	*sei*
seven	*sette*
eight	*otto*
nine	*nove*
ten	*dieci*
eleven	*undici*
twelve	*dodici*
thirteen	*tredici*
fourteen	*quattordici*
fifteen	*quindici*
sixteen	*sedici*
seventeen	*diciassette*
eighteen	*diciotto*
nineteen	*diciannove*
twenty	*venti*
a hundred	*cento*

A page for parents

I can read Italian is not intended to be a child's only source of Italian, but to be a supplement to other sources. For the child who knows no Italian it can be used in English, with occasional Italian words and phrases brought in as and when the parent feels the child can deal with them. In this way, the book can be used as a very gradual introduction to Italian. However, it will probably be more widely used by children who know a little Italian; and the following suggestions are given for such a child.

First of all, either the child reading the book, or a parent or friend, should know how to pronounce the Italian words in it. To get the greatest benefit the child should read the words aloud, and whenever necessary should be helped with pronunciation (see page 8). Many of the words reappear several times in the book, and if they are pronounced wrongly the first time, will be thoroughly but incorrectly learned by the end of the book.

The section **Gli amici di Timoteo** (pages 12 to 15) should be read first, as it introduces many characters who reappear throughout the book. After that, the sections can be read in any order as each is complete in itself. Children who know only very little Italian should start with the sections which have the smallest number of sentences, for example **Dall'elicottero** (page 32) and **In giardino al mattino presto** (page 48). Usually the sections in full colour contain a greater number of isolated words than the sections in two colours, many of which use sentences to tell a story.

After reading a few sections with both the Italian and the English visible, many children will enjoy going back to one section and testing their knowledge by covering up the English with a piece of paper, and seeing how much of the Italian they really know. The illustrations will help to show the meaning. The child should always study them when trying to find a meaning, rather than automatically refer to the English translation. If he works out the meaning for himself, and uses the translation only as a final check, he is far more likely to remember what he has learned.

Throughout the book, occasional questions are asked, to which the reader should be encouraged to give answers in Italian.

Its author hopes that *I can read Italian* will entertain and teach at one and the same time.